EASTER IN DURHAM

Bishop Jenkins and the Resurrection of Jesus

AUTHOR

Murray J Harris, MA, BD, PhD, is Warden of Tyndale House, a biblical research library in Cambridge. He is the author of Raised Immortal: Resurrection and Immortality in the New Testament, *published in the UK by Marshall, Morgan and Scott (1983) and in the USA by Wm B. Eerdmans (1985), which discusses in greater detail all the issues raised in the present essay.*

EASTER IN DURHAM

Bishop Jenkins and the Resurrection of Jesus

MURRAY J. HARRIS
Warden of Tyndale House, Cambridge

EXETER
THE PATERNOSTER PRESS

AUSTRALIA:
Bookhouse Australia Ltd.,
P.O. Box 115, Flemington Markets, NSW 2129

SOUTH AFRICA
Oxford University Press,
P.O. Box 1141, Cape Town

British Library Cataloguing in Publication Data

Harris, Murray J.
    Easter in Durham.
    1. Jesus Christ—Resurrection
    I. Title
    232'.5   BT481

ISBN 0-85364-419-5

Typeset in Great Britain by
Busby's Typesetting & Design, 52 Queen Street, Exeter, Devon
and printed for The Paternoster Press,
Paternoster House, 3 Mount Radford Crescent, Exeter, Devon
by Maslands Ltd., Tiverton.

CONTENTS

PREFACE

The present controversy over the Resurrection of Our Lord is of cardinal importance for the proclamation of the Christian Gospel. The New Testament portrays the Resurrection as the event through which the work of Jesus on the Cross bore fruit in what it describes as a new creation. To bear first-hand witness to the Resurrection was the first duty of the Apostles and the evidence that Jesus was raised in body, mind and spirit is set out in detail.

As Dr. Murray Harris makes clear in his excellent study, the ultimate point at issue is the authority of the Bible as a source of divine revelation and 'the touchstone of Christian doctrine, the bar at which all belief which claims to be Christian must be tested'.

To reduce the Resurrection to nothing more than an experience in the minds of the disciples is not only to challenge the authority of the Scriptures. It is also to challenge what they reveal about God. In the Bible he is both Creator of the universe and its Redeemer. It is significant that in his magisterial exposition of the Gospel in the Epistle to the Romans St. Paul begins with an affirmation of God as Creator before writing of what he has done in Christ. By the Resurrection man and the physical world, of which he is an integral part, are given a new potential and become capable of expressing the divine glory. Death and decay result in no more than the re-cycling of matter. In the Resurrection matter is given an ultimate place in God's design.

To see the Resurrection as no more than a spiritual experience is to abandon the biblical view and to pronounce a decree absolute between spirit and matter. Such an attitude conflicts both with the biblical teaching and, being based on an outdated positivism, with the modern scientific understanding of man as a psychosomatic unity. The deep and rich objective mystery of re-creation in Christ, which calls for the fullest exercise of all our faculties if we are to be grasped by its meaning, is replaced by a bloodless and subjective experience.

Dr. Harris's study is a model of how Christians should contend for 'the faith once delivered to the saints'. With courtesy and fairness, he allows the Bishop of Durham to speak for himself and directs his creative criticism towards what the Bishop has actually written or said. Dr. Harris has done us a great service and I commend his study warmly.

†GRAHAM LONDIN:

INTRODUCTION

There can be little doubt that the Bishop of Durham has often been misrepresented during the controversy over his views that has been swirling about in recent months. Impromptu and designedly provocative comments made in the course of brief interviews have been elevated to the status of sober theological affirmations, while sometimes he has been partially quoted, or quoted without regard to context, or simply misquoted. But public figures are used to such treatment.

Reaction to the Bishop's reported views has ranged from enthusiastic support to vigorous condemnation. He has been described, on the one hand, as a persecuted free-thinker or honest doubter, and on the other hand, as an insensitive pastor or outright heretic. Certainly more is at stake here than the right of individuals, whether public or private figures, to hold distinctive views about sport or economics or politics or religion. Like all bishops of the Church of England, Dr Jenkins is pledged to "believe ... expound and teach" the doctrine of the Christian faith "which is revealed in the holy Scriptures" (quoted from the Order of Service for the Ordination of a Bishop, Alternative Services Book). So whenever he speaks on religious matters he is a representative, if not a spokesman, of the Church of England. This makes it all the more important that his views are represented accurately so that they may be examined fairly. Yet it should also be noted that Bishop Jenkins is not alone in holding the views he expresses, for similar views of the resurrection are shared by many theologians and church leaders.

What this booklet seeks to do is to state as carefully as possible, often in the Bishop's own words, his views on the resurrection of Jesus, already expressed by him in writing before the present controversy began. As he himself put it: "It might make a very valuable contribution to rebuilding communication, trust and community in our divided society if Christians always exercised great restraint in responding to all media events and relied on patient inquiry before they reacted to them" (from his written statement, dated 22nd May 1984, addressed "to those who wish to form a Christian judgement about the controversy which has arisen over my remarks on recent T.V. programmes"). The present aim, then, is to give an accurate description of his views on the resurrection of Jesus after the necessary "patient inquiry", before attempting to assess those views in the light of the New Testament records.

The present writer recognises that the ultimate point at issue in the controversy is the authority of the Bible as a source of divine revelation: is it, or is it not, the touchstone of Christian doctrine, the bar at which all belief which claims to be Christian must be tested? But there is a further reason for our present preoccupation with what the New Testament says about the resurrection. The data of the New Testament provide the earliest Christian tradition about Jesus' resurrection. In fact, were it not for the New Testament claims about the resurrection of Jesus, we would lack any sure knowledge at all of how the earliest Christians regarded this occurrence.

My sources for the Bishop's views are the following books written by him, here listed in order of publication and with the abbreviations hereafter used.

Jesus and God (co-author, G.B. Caird) (London: Faith, 1965) (Jesus)

The Glory of Man (London: SCM, 1967) (Glory)

Living with Questions (London: SCM, 1969) (Questions)

What is Man? (London: SCM, 1970) (Man)

The Contradiction of Christianity (London: SCM, 1976) (Contradiction)

Reference will also be made to four other more recent sources:

Credo programme, 29th April 1984 (copyright of London Weekend Television) (Credo)

"Poles Apart", BBC Radio 4 programme, 28th October 1984 (copyright of the BBC) ("Poles")

"The meaning of Easter", in The Durham Lamp (Monthly Newsletter of Durham Diocese), April 1985 pp.2-3 ("Easter").

"Gospel stories were written to convey a message" in Church of England Newspaper and British Weekly, 4th April 1985, p.8 ("Gospel stories").

For the sake of clarity, but at the risk of over-simplification, we may characterise the Bishop's views about the resurrection of Jesus in five statements, which we shall then amplify, often in his own words, before undertaking an appraisal.

1

WHO EXPERIENCED THE RESURRECTION?

The Bishop's view

The resurrection of Jesus was a series of events demonstrating the "livingness" of Jesus and experienced by the disciples of Jesus, not a single event experienced by Jesus (a view most clearly expressed in the *Credo* programme).

Over a period of time and through a variety of experiences the followers of Jesus became convinced that although Jesus had died and been buried, "he wasn't finished". On the contrary he was "raised up" in that God had "established him in his person, in his achievements, and in his continuing significance" (*Questions*, p.138; and in particular, *Credo*). By his death "Jesus ... may have been brought to nothing but he was not reduced to nothing", because at different times and in different ways there came to his disciples "the experienced discovery of his risenness" and through this the discovery that he was the Messiah (*Glory*, p.86, cf. "Gospel stories").

"The relevant records indicate that Jesus was first decisively, rather than tentatively, recognized as the Messiah when a comparative handful of people among those who had been associated with him became convinced that the cross on which he had died had not terminated the pattern and the purpose of Jesus' life. Their conviction, based on evidence which they seemed to some extent to be able to share and to discuss and recognize in common, was that 'God had raised him up'. They believed they had evidence that the understanding, commitment and direction of the life of Jesus had not terminated in his death on the cross, but was continued in his livingness, known to his immediate followers and to be made known as widely as possible in the world at large" (*Glory*, p.32).

From this we may infer that the resurrection of Jesus, "his livingness", was the continuation of the pattern and purpose of his life in the experience of his followers. We should therefore not identify the resurrection with a single event that occurred on Easter morning (*Credo*).

Appraisal

In any attempt to assess these views it is important to know how the term "resurrection" is used in the New Testament. We find there no fewer than five types of resurrection:

(1) the past restoration to physical life of isolated individuals (e.g., Mark 5:41-42);

(2) the past bodily resurrection of Christ to immortality (e.g., Rom. 6:9);

(3) the past spiritual resurrection of believers with Christ (e.g., Col. 2:12);

(4) the future bodily resurrection of believers to immortality (e.g., 1 Cor. 15:52);

(5) the future personal resurrection of unbelievers to judgment (e.g., Acts 24:15).

What is significant here is that resurrection is never a process; the present tense of verbs that describe the act of raising or rising is never found in the New Testament. Nor, in reference to a single individual, is resurrection ever a series of events, whether those events be considered separately or as a unit. Rather, resurrection is everywhere regarded as a single event that leads to a state. Christians were corporately "raised with Christ" (event) and so are "alive from the dead" (state) (Colossians 3:1; Romans 6:13). In the future as well, the resurrection event produces the resurrected state: "we shall be raised immortal" (1 Corinthians 15:52). Similarly, the resurrection of Jesus is depicted as a single past event ("he rose", *egerthe* or *aneste*) and consequently as a present state ("he is risen", *egegertai*; "risen", *egegermenos*) (e.g., 1 Corinthians 15:12; 2 Corinthians 5:15; 2 Timothy 2:8).

Confirmation of this point is found in the expression "on the third day" which is often attached to the verb "be raised", "rise", in reference to Jesus' resurrection (e.g., Matthew 16:21; Luke 24:7). If his resurrection amounted to a succession of events, it would make no sense to add that it occurred at a specific time, "on the third day". Yet one of the four ingredients in the earliest Christian preaching was the confession: "He was raised on the third day" (1 Corinthians 15:4).

There are two main ways in which New Testament writers speak of Jesus' resurrection: "God raised Jesus" (e.g., Acts 3:15; Romans 10:9) and "Jesus rose" or "Jesus was raised" (e.g., Mark 16:6; 1 Thessalonians 4:14). The Bishop distinctly prefers the first expression, and rarely, if ever, uses the latter two, which is significant, for to say that "Jesus rose" makes it unambiguous that Jesus is the subject of the action: the resurrection happened to Jesus. It was not simply the case that God acted on Jesus'

11

disciples to convince them of "his livingness on the other side of his death" (*Glory*, p.98).

Far from being a subjective awareness that had been instilled in the minds of the disciples by God, the resurrection was an objective occurrence involving the person of Jesus. The "many compelling signs" or "many convincing proofs" mentioned in Acts 1:3 were not a series of individual testimonies to an inward conviction that Jesus was alive but a series of appearances during a forty-day period when Jesus "presented himself alive after his passion". We cannot agree with Bishop Jenkins that "the evidence of the resurrection is the faith of the apostles and the subsequent faith" ("Poles").

The testimony of the New Testament is unambiguous. The resurrection was a single event experienced by Jesus that was followed by a series of events—his appearances—that were witnessed by his disciples.

2

WHAT WAS REAL?

The Bishop's view

The resurrection of Jesus was real and is a fact of the past, in that Jesus' presence, power and influence actually did persist through and beyond death.

Some of the first disciples knew Jesus as a person, "the shape of Jesus in his living ... Some of them were well aware of the shape of Jesus' dying ... Some of them were equally aware of a new living of Jesus, a living as real and actual as the living of Jesus from Nazareth to the cross and a living as much present, and as much to be reckoned with, as the dying, becoming a corpse and being buried ... The burying was real and the being alive again was real and that in the same categories of reality" (*Questions*, p.137; similarly *Glory*, p.23). People were not simply reaping the benefits of wish-fulfilment when they declared Jesus "risen". The resurrection was not caused by the vivid or desperate imagination or pious wishes of Jesus' disciples (*Credo*; "Gospel stories"), nor had they spontaneously persuaded themselves that Jesus was "as good as alive". But if "God enabled some men to perceive the lasting significance of the shape of Jesus' personality", we are presented with the resurrection as "a fact of the past", for "to cause a belief, and *a fortiori* to cause a true belief, is just as much a happening as, say, raising up Jesus" (*Questions*, p.138).

Appraisal

We welcome the Bishop's insistence on the reality of the resurrection, that it was no figment of the disciples' imagination. But at issue here is not the question whether the resurrection was real and factual—the early church would have endorsed this verdict wholeheartedly. The question is *what* was real and *to whom* it was real.

For the Bishop, what was real was the "new living of Jesus", his "being alive again". For the early Christians, what was real was first of all the coming-to-life-again of Jesus and then his risen life (e.g., Romans 8:34; 1 Peter 3:21-22). They would not have hesitated to call Jesus' resurrection "a fact of the past", but for them the fact was not simply that "the pattern and purpose of Jesus' life" continued in spite of his death (*Glory*, p.32). The prior and foundational fact was that the Jesus who had been crucified and placed in a tomb had been rescued by God from the ravages of death and restored to life in a resuscitated and transformed body (Acts 2:23-24, 31-32; 13:29-31). All the emphasis in the Bishop's discussion is on Jesus' "livingness" (as he terms it) and the disciples' discovery and awareness of this. What he neglects, perhaps because of its materialistic overtones, is what we might call the "rising-ness" of Jesus, his actual return from death to life. After all, in its basic meaning, "resurrection" denotes "restoration to life", not "life"; a "rising up" from the tomb and death, not "being alive again". It is not the case that the early Christians first believed that "Jesus is alive" and subsequently claimed that "Jesus rose". Rather, the opposite was true. They knew that "Jesus rose" and therefore confidently affirmed that "Jesus is alive".

Moreover, Bishop Jenkins sees the resurrection as real principally, if not exclusively, to the disciples. "Some of them were ... aware of a new living of Jesus, ... a living as much present, and as much to be reckoned with, as the dying" (*Questions*, p.137; cf. "Easter", p.3). One wonders whether the Bishop would be willing to affirm that the resurrection was as real an event *for Jesus himself* as was his death. Here, as elsewhere, we detect a failure to distinguish the reactions of the disciples from the prior experience of Jesus. Jesus had, in reality, been resurrected before his disciples discovered it to be really so (e.g., Luke 24:1-49).

Bishop Jenkins insists not only that the resurrection was as real, as much a happening, as the burial, but that this was so "in the same categories of reality". We would readily grant that, on this view, God's causing a true belief to lodge in the disciples' mind would be as much an historical event as Joseph of Arimathea's burial of Jesus in a tomb, but it is difficult to see how these two events would be "in the same categories of reality". One was indubitably an external event, something that was done *to* the subject and therefore was open to empirical verification, the other was, on this view, a psychological or spiritual phenomenon, something that occurred *within* certain subjects and therefore was not capable of being verified empirically.

The resurrection was basically God's restoration of Jesus to life, not God's perpetuation of the personal impact of Jesus or the disciples' discovery and awareness of his "livingness". The resurrection was a real experience for Jesus himself before it became a real conviction of his disciples.

14

3

WHAT KIND OF MIRACLE?

The Bishop's view

The resurrection of Jesus was, in the final analysis, caused by God and may not inappropriately be termed both a miracle and a mystery.

We cannot describe the resurrection as simply the natural continuation of the influence of Jesus or merely a sense of his continuing presence (as when a friend dies), for "God was somehow involved in producing this event" (*Credo*), "God had directed his [Jesus'] new living" (*Questions*, p.137), "God enabled some men to perceive the lasting significance of the shape of Jesus' personality" (*Questions*, p.138). "The Resurrection means that God acted to establish Jesus in his person, in his achievements and in his continuing effect" (*Questions*, p.139).

In "a short theological word-book of the Bible", entitled *Bible Meanings*, written by Dr. Jenkins, H. Graydon and E.C.D. Stanford (London: OUP, 1963), the resurrection of Jesus is defined as "the act of God which convinced the disciples that Jesus who had been dead was alive and effective for them and for all men" (p.54). If one may use the term "miracle" in this context, the resurrection may be said to be miraculous in that, at divine prompting, the apostles and others came to believe that the power, purpose and presence of Jesus were continuing "both in the sphere of God and in the sphere of history". Yet this divine action does not rule out the operation of "some, as it were, quasi-physical, quasi-psychological causes" (*Credo*). What is more, the resurrection is a mystery as well as a miracle. Whenever we are confronted with a claim that the transcendent God has acted in the physical universe, we are entering a realm of mystery and faith where precise explanations and exact descriptions are impossible ("Poles"). "You cannot tell precisely what happened at the first Easter nor get behind the experiences, encounters and discoveries of the early Church and their way of telling the stories of Faith" ("Gospel stories").

Appraisal

There can be no doubt that the New Testament emphasises that God was the cause of the resurrection of Jesus. The phrase "God raised him (up)" is common (e.g. Acts 2:24,32; 5:30; 13:30; 1 Corinthians 6:14), so that in the passive voice, "Jesus was raised", God is clearly the implied agent. This conclusion is not materially altered by such complementary statements as that Jesus was raised "by the glory of the Father" (Romans 6:4) or rose by his own power (John 2:19-21; 10:17-18). But again the crucial issue is: *what* did God cause? Against Professor Jenkins' insistence that it was the disciples' settled conviction about Jesus' "risenness" that God caused, we would urge that it was the reanimation and transformation of a buried corpse. Just as we must make a clear distinction between the single, initial act of God (viz. the resurrection of Jesus) and the subsequent responses of Jesus' followers, so we must also clearly distinguish that initial divine act from the various means God used to bring the disciples to recognise the reality of Jesus' resurrection. The resurrection narratives mention at least four means.

(i) *The empty tomb as interpreted by the angelic messengers.* In itself the empty tomb was ambiguous testimony; its discovery led to perplexity, doubt and awe (Luke 24:3-4, 12; Mark 16:8) as well as faith (John 20:8). But the angel's announcement provided the definitive explanation of the empty tomb: "He is not here; for he has risen" (Matthew 28:5-6).

(ii) *The post-resurrection appearances of Jesus.* These personal encounters with the risen Jesus regularly resulted in faith and worship (Matthew 28:9, 17; John 20:26-28), although they sometimes prompted initial fear or doubt (Matthew 28:17; Luke 24:36-38).

(iii) *The testimony of eyewitnesses of the empty tomb and the resurrected Lord.* Again, such reports were often greeted with amazement or outright scepticism (Luke 24:11, 22-24) but their significance grew with the passage of time (John 20:18,29).

(iv) *Reflection on messianic prophecy* (Luke 24:22-27, 44-46; John 20:3-9) *and on Jesus' predictions of his resurrection* (Mark 8:31; 9:31; 10:32-34).

On almost any definition of miracle, the resurrection of Jesus, however interpreted, would be deemed miraculous. Whether we follow C.S. Lewis and define a miracle as "an interference with Nature by supernatural power" (*Miracles*, London, Collins, 1947, p.9), or, better, regard a miracle as a self-revelatory act of God of an unusual or unexpected kind (that is, not conforming to what is understood of nature) which is designed to prompt faith, the resurrection qualifies for this description. The Fourth Evangelist seems to have regarded both the resurrection and the resurrection appearances of Jesus as "signs" (John 20:30), miraculous occurrences that pointed beyond themselves to spiritual truths about Jesus. But unlike the Bishop, we would regard the resurrection as being principally a physical miracle rather than a purely psychological or spiritual miracle.

We happily concur in the Bishop's use of the term "mystery" in connection with the resurrection, but once more we differ in the reasons for approving of the term. While he believes that at the point where God's action intersects with the material world, a certain imprecision of description and mysteriousness always remain, we maintain that efforts to describe divine action in the universe, especially when those efforts are divinely inspired and directed, need not be in any way imprecise or inexact. Whereas he believes that "the Gospels are not careful, literal, news-like accounts of a set of events" ("Poles") but rather were written "to express faith and to convey a particular message or answer to a particular question" ("Gospel stories"), we maintain that there is no need to "get behind" the experiences of the early Christians or to unravel the mystery of "their way of telling the stories of Faith" before arriving at trustworthy information about the resurrection. We do not deny that the resurrection narratives, like the Gospels as a whole, are confessional history and reflect the Church in its preaching, teaching and worship. But this apologetic and theological purpose need not—indeed, does not—prejudice the historical reliability of the narratives. The "mystery" of the resurrection lies in another area, we believe.

In its full Christian sense, resurrection signifies more than mere *resuscitation*, the regaining of the life forfeited through death. It also involves *transformation*, the alteration or enhancement of the properties of the physical body. In his resurrected body, Jesus was no longer bound by material or spatial limitations (e.g., John 20:19,26), his essential state was one of invisibility and therefore immateriality (Luke 24:31,36) and he could materialise and therefore be localised at will (Luke 24:39-40; John 20:27). No longer was he subject to death (Romans 6:9; Revelation 1:18). The resurrection marked Jesus' entrance upon a spiritual mode of existence, or, to borrow Paul's expression, his acquisition of a "spiritual body" (1 Corinthians 15:44).

But resurrection also implies *exaltation*. By his resurrection Jesus was exalted to God's "right hand", the place of unique honour and power (Acts 2:32-33; 3:13,15; 5:30-31; Ephesians 1:20; Hebrews 10:12; 1 Peter 3:22). While the revival and metamorphosis of Jesus of Nazareth after his crucifixion and burial are open to historical enquiry, his exaltation to the right hand of God is a tenet of faith that is not susceptible to historical investigation. As a three-dimensional event that occurred simultaneously within history and beyond history, the resurrection of Jesus may be aptly termed a "mystery".

God was the sole cause of the raising and transformation of Jesus' body and his exaltation, but there were several mediate causes, under God, that finally prompted the conviction among the disciples that Jesus was alive and active, albeit in an enhanced bodily state.

4

WAS IT A BODILY RESURRECTION?

The Bishop's view

The resurrection of Jesus was a personal resurrection but not a bodily resurrection.

In his passion and death, Jesus was "submerged in the destructiveness of evil" (*Glory*, p.89), but by the resurrection God established Jesus in his person, that is, preserved and declared his identity. By this Bishop Jenkins means that God re-established "the shape of Jesus Christ", "the person that he was, the expectations which he aroused and the promises which were thereby held out". God, "the establisher of identity", reaffirmed the continuing effect of Jesus "in his own personal pattern and presence, through and beyond death ... It was Jesus who was known to be living again, not the spirit of Christ, nor the essence of love nor the embodiment of humanity" (*Questions*, pp.139, 140; also *Jesus*, p.32; *Glory*, pp.98-99). Jesus endured evil but then emerged from evil "as a distinctive, living and personal activity. The Logos of the cosmos is not a mythological theory but a crucified man" (*Glory*, p.89).

The Bishop avers that he is unsure whether the story of the empty tomb symbolised the belief that Jesus was alive or whether the incident was one of the events that caused belief in the resurrection (*Questions*, p.137; *Glory*, p.32; "Easter", p.2). Either way, there was and is no resurrection body of Jesus apart from "the body of Christ", the Church. To the apostle Paul's question "With what body will the dead come?" there can be only one answer: "they will come with the body and in the body of Jesus Christ" (*Questions*, pp.140-141).

> Men come to know God as they throw in their lot with the people of God. And it is no mere figure of speech ... to speak of the people of God as the body of Christ; for this is the place where Jesus is embodied now, where he is to be encountered, where he is not only still alive—for he is alive everywhere—but where he is known to be alive (*Jesus*, p.81).

Appraisal

Bishop Jenkins rightly recognises that the very notion of resurrection implies an element of continuity between the "before" and the "after". He depicts this continuity as personal, not physical or material or bodily. It was in rejecting any idea of a "literally physical" resurrection of Jesus, of a "resuscitated corpse", that he made his celebrated comment about a "conjuring trick with bones". "After all, a conjuring trick with bones only proves that someone is clever at a conjuring trick with bones" ("Poles").

But the evidence of the New Testament demands we affirm that the resurrection of Jesus was both personal and bodily. The risen Jesus was precisely the same person as Jesus of Nazareth, with identity of personal characteristics in areas such as memory, disposition, attitudes, diction and habits. The angelic declaration was "You seek Jesus of Nazareth who was crucified. He has risen" (Mark 16:6). Jesus' resurrection body was not a fresh creation of God, a "creation out of nothing". Jesus was recognised by his followers when he appeared to them after his resurrection because of such features as his tone of voice (John 20:16), his bodily movements (Luke 24:30-31, 35), and the marks of the crucifixion (Luke 24:39-40; John 20:27).

But there was sometimes difficulty in recognising the risen Jesus, not only because of distance or dimness of light (John 20:14-15; 21:4), the suddenness and unexpectedness of his appearances (Luke 24:36-37), and the disciples' preoccupation with grief and perplexity (Luke 24:18-24; John 20:11-15), but also because of his altered bodily form. Since the physical body of Jesus that had been buried had gained, as the result of a resurrection transformation, the properties of a spiritual body, we cannot say that the resurrected Jesus had precisely the same body as Jesus of Nazareth. That on which God worked in effecting a resurrection transformation was nothing other than the buried body of Jesus, but the outcome was that the same person occupied a different dwelling, so to speak. There had been a metamorphosis of his body. From the empty tomb we learn that there was an ineradicable element of bodily continuity; the appearances, on the other hand, show that there was an ineradicable element of bodily discontinuity. As we have already shown, in his risen state Jesus transcended the normal laws of physical existence. Yet in this change into a spiritual mode of existence (what Paul calls a "spiritual body", 1 Corinthians 15:44) Jesus' personal identity remained intact. It was a case of bodily transformation yet personal identity. So we see that a physical resurrection need not involve what Bishop

Jenkins calls "a conjuring trick with bones". If the actual body of Jesus was raised and transformed, there was no "trick" involving the removal of a corpse to produce an empty tomb.

One must seriously question whether, on the Bishop's view, the risen Jesus was "personal" in any real and individual sense. In describing Jesus' post-resurrection state he uses the curious—and revealing—phrase "a distinctive living and personal *activity*" (*Glory*, p.89; italics mine). When he asserts that "it was Jesus who was known to be living again, not the spirit of Christ, nor the essence of love nor the embodiment of humanity" (*Questions*, p.140), it is not the case that he is arguing for the personal identity between Jesus of Nazareth and the resurrected Jesus but rather for an identity between the Jesus experienced by the disciples before his death and the Jesus experienced by them after his "resurrection".

But perhaps the most conclusive piece of evidence that the Bishop fails to affirm an actually personal resurrection of Jesus is his equation of the resurrection body of Jesus with the Church. "The body of Christ ... is the place where Jesus is embodied now" (*Jesus*, p.81). Once a person denies the bodily resurrection of Jesus from the grave, the way is open to equate the Church with the risen body of Jesus. On the other hand, once we give full weight to the testimony of the New Testament and so allow an individual resurrection body of Jesus, there can be no such equation or else there would be two resurrection bodies of Jesus Christ. As the "body of Christ", the Church is the principal means by which the risen Christ expresses himself on earth, but it is not his sole "embodiment". There is oneness and solidarity, but not identity, between the risen Christ and his Church. The description of the risen Jesus as the "head of the body, the Church" (Colossians 1:18; cf. 2:19) or "head of the Church, his body" (Ephesians 5:23; cf. 1:22-23; 4:15-16) not only affirms that Jesus is inseparable from the Church but also excludes his identity with it. In addition, Paul speaks of the resurrected body of Jesus as "his glorious body", the pattern for the resurrection transformation of believers' bodies (Philippians 3:20-21), and in 1 Corinthians 15:42-49 he draws a series of contrasts between Adam, the man of dust, and Christ, the man from heaven, one contrast being the difference between Adam's "physical body" (which is characterised by perishability, dishonour and weakness) and Christ's "spiritual body" (which is characterised by imperishability, glory and power).

The New Testament records leave us in no doubt that on the first Easter morning the tomb where Jesus had been buried was empty (apart, that is, from the burial linens, that prompted at least one disciple to believe, John 20:3-5, 8). Six converging lines of evidence support this conclusion.

First, the tradition of the empty tomb is found in all four Gospels, which reflect several separate strata of material—Mark (16:1-8), Matthew's special material (28:11-15), John (20:11-18), and probably Luke (24:1-12).

Secondly, the earliest account of the discovery of the empty tomb, that found in Mark 16:1-8, is remarkably restrained and unadorned. The account contains no description of the actual rising of Jesus, no indication of the excitement of the witnesses at their discovery, and no attempt to introduce theological motifs such as the fulfilment of Old Testament prophecy. If Mark's record were a legendary fabrication, we might have expected the narrative to be adorned with fantastic features befitting an event which, if true, must from any perspective have been the most stupendous occurrence in human history. Legendary features are clearly evident in such later Christian writing about the resurrection as the Gospel of Peter (mid-second century A.D.). With its extraordinary sobriety, Mark's narrative has the "ring of truth".

Thirdly, the earliest dispute between Jews and Christians concerning the resurrection of Jesus of which we have a record (Matthew 28:11-15) shows that the point at issue was not the fact of the empty tomb but its significance. It is inconceivable that when the Christians publicly claimed in Jerusalem that "the God of Abraham and of Isaac and of Jacob" had overturned the Jewish rejection of Jesus by raising him from the dead (Acts 2:23-24; 3:13-15; 4:10; 5:30) the Jerusalem Jews would have maintained a conspiracy of silence if they had proof that the tomb was still occupied or could produce witnesses who could account for the disappearance and disposal of the body. The bold and startling claim of the Christians would have collapsed if someone in the audience could retort, "We know where Jesus was buried, and we have checked—the tomb is still intact", or "Here are witnesses who know the whereabouts of Jesus' body". The claim that the tomb was empty was open to what some call "empirical falsification".

Fourthly, the gospels depict women as the first witnesses of the empty tomb (e.g., Mark 16:1-6), yet in Jewish law the testimony of women was inadmissible as evidence. If the story of the empty tomb were merely an apologetic legend or the work of a fabricator, we should have expected the witnesses to be exclusively men and the first witnesses to be apostles.

Fifthly, in the light of Jewish veneration for the burial-places of prophets and righteous martyrs (Matthew 23:29), the apparent disregard of the tomb of Jesus by the early Christians is best explained by the assumption that it was empty.

Sixthly, to Jews of the first century A.D., any idea of a resurrection shortly after death involved the emptying of a tomb or grave, the revival of the physical body. The Jewish contemporaries of Jesus knew that Lazarus could not be raised from the dead until first the stone that lay over his burial cave had been removed (John 11:38-44). No one could be regarded as resurrected while his corpse lay in a tomb. So the early Christian claim that Jesus was alive necessarily implied that his body was no longer entombed. Accordingly, when Paul asserts, on the one hand, that Jesus was "laid in a tomb" (Acts 13:29) or was buried (1 Corinthians 15:4), and on the other, that he had been raised from the dead (Acts 13:30; 1 Corinthians 15:4), he is implying that the sepulchre in which he had been buried was empty. Paul's silence about the empty tomb is more apparent than real. Between Jesus' burial and his appearances there must lie, for any first-century Jew, a bodily resurrection from the grave (1 Corinthians 15:4-5). In any case, it is hard to believe that when Paul conferred with Peter in Jerusalem regarding early Christian traditions (Galatians 1:18) mention was not made of Peter's discovery of the empty tomb (Luke 24:12; John 20:3-10). Our ignorance of the extent of Paul's knowledge does not amount to knowledge of the extent of his ignorance.

Now it is clear that in itself an empty tomb proves nothing more than that the tomb is empty; here we agree with the Bishop ("Easter", p.3). If, for instance, a corpse were to go missing from a mortuary, the empty mortuary would in itself be no evidence of resurrection. Considered by itself, the empty tomb was ambiguous testimony, capable of several different interpretations, as John 20:1-2, 8, 11-15 makes clear. But the empty tomb was, in fact, not "by itself". As we have already seen, there was, on the one hand, the definitive divine explanation of the emptiness given by the interpreting angel, "He has risen, he is not here; see the place where they laid him" (Mark 16:6), an interpretation that confirmed scriptural predictions of the Messiah's resurrection (Luke 24:22-27; John 20:3-9; 1 Corinthians 15:4), and on the other hand, the repeated appearances of the risen Jesus to individuals and groups, to men and women, in both Jerusalem and Galilee, during a six-week period (e.g.: John 20:11-29; 21:1-22; Acts 1:3; 13:31). From this triad of evidences—empty tomb, divine interpretation, and resurrection appearances—only one possible inference could be drawn: Jesus had risen from the grave.

That these appearances were not *subjective visions* but

genuine external encounters between persons, involving physical visibility (appearing and being seen), is evident from the following observations.

(1) The verbal form most commonly used to describe a resurrection appearance (viz. *ophthe*) means "he appeared", in the sense of "he came into visibility", "he let himself be seen" (e.g., Luke 24:34; Acts 9:17; 1 Corinthians 15:5-8). Had the New Testament writers wanted to express the idea that Jesus "appeared" in a manner resembling a person's appearance in a dream, another verb would have been used (viz. *phainomai*). Moreover, it is significant that the term "vision" (*horama* or *optasia*) is not found in the gospel records of Jesus' appearances.

(2) Those to whom Jesus appeared were said to "see" him or to "recognise" him (e.g., Matthew 28:7,17; Luke 24:31; John 20:14,18,20,29), where the normal verbs denoting visual recognition are used.

(3) When Jesus appeared he was not only seen but also heard (Luke 24:25-27; John 21:15-18; Acts 1:3) and touched (Matthew 28:9; cf. Luke 24:37-40; John 20:25,27). To assure the disciples of his reality he even took food (Luke 24:38-43).

(4) The disciples were not in a psychological condition that was conducive to hallucinations. So far from being full of expectancy and absorbed in meditation, they had gathered behind locked doors (John 20:19), were immersed in gloom (Luke 24:17,21), and greeted the first news of the resurrection as "sheer nonsense" (Luke 24:11). In any case, an hallucination is an individual, private occurrence (contrast the gospel record of Jesus' appearance to groups; e.g., Matthew 28:16-17; John 20:19-29; 21:1-22); one may ask whether simultaneous, identical hallucinations are psychologically feasible.

No more likely is the theory that God induced *objective visions* of Jesus in the consciousness of Jesus' disciples to convince them that his resurrection was a spiritual reality. God can scarcely be acquitted of duplicity in initiating such "telegrams from heaven" (as they have been called) if there was no correspondence between what was "seen" (viz. Jesus in some recognisable and therefore bodily form) and what was actually true (viz. his body was decaying in some grave in Jerusalem or else had been disposed of by burning).

The most satisfactory explanation of the empty tomb of Jesus is that his body was raised. Those who reject a physical resurrection are obliged to posit one of the following unconvincing hypotheses: that Jesus merely swooned on the cross and then recovered in the cool tomb; that the women visited the wrong tomb; that Jesus' body was stolen, either by his disciples or by his enemies; that his body was placed in a common grave or was burned on the rubbish heaps outside Jerusalem or was cremated by his disciples, hypotheses which require that both the burial narrative and the empty tomb narrative be dismissed as literary creations; that we do not or cannot know what happened to his body. When Dr. Jenkins describes the proposal that the disciples stole the body as "the alternative rational and plausible explanation" ("Easter", p.3), he is overlooking several insuperable objections to such an explanation. How did the disciples manage to elude or overpower the guard of Jewish temple police that had been posted at the tomb precisely to prevent such a robbery (Matthew 27:62-66)? Why would anyone stealing the body bother to unwind and then fold or rewind the several yards of linen cloth that encircled the corpse (cf. John 20:6-7)? Moreover, it is difficult enough to believe that dispirited disciples who were oblivious of Jesus' predictions of his resurrection (Mark 8:31-32; Luke 24:6-8,11) would fix on the desperate plan of stealing the body, vowing never to divulge the truth and proclaiming his resurrection. But it stretches credulity beyond the limit to believe that men were willing to suffer and die for what they knew to be a gigantic hoax and that the truth never slipped out, even to other followers of Jesus.

In addition to the testimony of the resurrection narratives themselves, there are several reasons why Christians should affirm the bodily resurrection of Jesus.

(1) On some 30 occasions in the New Testament, the phrase "from the dead" is added to the expression "God raised Jesus" or "Jesus rose". Acts 13:29-30 makes it clear that in the case of Jesus' resurrection, "from the dead" means "from the tomb": "They took him (Jesus) down from the tree, and laid him in a tomb. But God raised him from the dead" (see also Acts 2:29-32).

(2) In their preaching both Peter (Acts 2:24-32) and Paul (Acts 13:34-37) insisted that the resurrection occurred before the body of Jesus began to decompose: whereas King David's body did "see corruption", God did not allow "his Holy One" to "see corruption". Such insistence is relevant only if Jesus' actual body was resurrected.

(3) Paul believed that the resurrection of Jesus forms the pattern for the resurrection of believers (1 Corinthians 15:20,23). This does not imply that the two resurrections are identical in every respect so that we can argue from the Gospels to the Epistles or vice-versa with regard to the nature and significance of the two; for instance, Jesus was raised "on the third day" (1 Corinthians 15:4), not on the Last Day, and "for

our justification" (Romans 4:25). With this said, it is clear from 1 Corinthians 15:42-44 and 2 Corinthians 5:1-2 that Paul conceived of believers' resurrection state as an embodied state, and therefore, since it was a prototype, Christ's resurrected state must also have been viewed as one of embodiment.

(4) The Fourth Evangelist believed that Jesus' prophecy that he would "raise up" the destroyed temple "within three days" was fulfilled when "the temple of his body" was raised from the dead on the third day (John 2:19-22).

5

FOR WHOM—AND WHEN?

The Bishop's view

The resurrection of Jesus guarantees that all persons will ultimately be established and fulfilled in their personal identity through membership of the community of Jesus Christ, so that resurrection is a fact of the future as well as a fact of the past. Moreover, in bridging past and future, resurrection is a present reality.

"The Resurrection is a preservation of identity and a declaration of identity. In raising up Jesus, God makes it plain that his resources are at work for, and are at the disposal of, the establishment, development and liberation of human identity." But identity implies community; we are to be fulfilled not as mere individuals but as the people of God. "The resurrection of Jesus promises that I shall be me, but only and excellently in oneness with all men" (*Questions*, pp.139-140). At present people are either emergent loving persons or potentially emergent loving persons, but in the consummated Kingdom of God "we shall all be perfected through the perfections of one another" (*Man*, p.118) and receive "the fullness of the life of God in unimpeded relations with him and with one another" (*Contradiction*, p.23). In a universe which "is the experiment of a power, presence and purpose who is rightly understood in terms of love" (*Man*, p.106), man is emerging into the image of God who is love (*Man*, pp.107, 112) so that "our future is God" (*Man*, p.113). Yet we must remain agnostic about the nature of the fulfilment of the work of love in eternity, "although we may guess something through our experiences of the depths of love. Thus we really have nothing to say about that which is symbolized and pointed to by such phrases as 'the resurrection of the body and the life everlasting' " (*Man*, p.114).

Being a fact of both the future and the past, resurrection must also have a present existence. "The reality of the Resurrection should be looked out for and expected wherever we are offered possibilities of, or faced with problems about, identity and community. This is where we shall find possibilities of dying and rising, of being brought to an end and of discovering offers of new beginnings which are reflections and realizations of the power of the Resurrection ... Every development of community is itself a sign of the Resurrection" (*Questions*, p.141).

Appraisal

Here we may register some partial agreement with the Bishop, but as elsewhere the areas of disagreement are more fundamental than those of agreement.

First, we concur that the resurrection of Jesus is the "firstfruits" (1 Corinthians 15:20,23), guaranteeing the final ingathering of the full Easter harvest of resurrected persons. Jesus was not merely "the first to rise from the dead" (Acts 26:23) with immortal life (Romans 6:9); his rising foreshadows and guarantees the resurrection of the righteous. "Through the power of Jesus God will bring with him (i.e. by virtue of association with the risen Jesus) those who have fallen asleep" (1 Thessalonians 4:14). As certainly as the harvest follows the firstfruits, the resurrection of the members of the Body will follow the resurrection of the Head. But the point to notice here is that when Paul uses the analogy of firstfruits and harvest, the whole, of which the resurrection of Jesus Christ is the first part and the pledge, is the resurrection of "those who belong to Christ" (1 Corinthians 15:23), that is, believers in Christ. The fact that Jesus rose from the dead guarantees that all persons will be judged by him "in righteousness" (Acts 17:31), not that all will share his resurrection to immortal life in God's presence. We must distinguish the resurrection of the just (Luke 14:14) from the resurrection of the unjust (Acts 24:15).

Secondly, no one can doubt that in the New Testament resurrection is seen as future as well as past. In the summary of New Testament usage given above (see p.11), we saw that the resurrection of believers to immortality and of unbelievers to judgment lay in the future. Indeed, many commentators believe that in 1 Corinthians 15, the great death-resurrection chapter, the apostle Paul is seeking to establish two basic points against those Corinthian proto-gnostics who held that the resurrection of believers, accomplished in baptism, was spiritual and was past: the resurrection of believers is bodily, not spiritual; future, not past. But to acknowledge that resurrection is both past and future is not to affirm that it is a present occurrence. The New Testament never depicts resurrection as an ongoing experience or process. By its very nature resurrection is an event, leading to a state. Christians were "made alive together with Christ" (Ephesians 2:5) and so are in a state of spiritual resurrection ("alive from the dead", Romans 6:13) and are being progressively transformed into Christ's image (2 Corinthians 3:18), not progressively raised. In fact, resurrection may be spoken of as the acceleration and completion of the process of becoming like Christ (e.g., Romans 8:29). It is only because the Bishop roots Jesus' resurrection in the experience of the disciples and not in any significant sense in the experience of Jesus that he can reinterpret the term "resurrection" as a symbol for recurring religious or community experience.

Thirdly, we agree that resurrection is a corporate notion. The New Testament never suggests that in the hereafter resurrected individuals enjoy the beatific vision in fellowship with Christ but in "splendid isolation" from one another. While the resurrection may be experienced individually, it is the whole host of the righteous dead that is raised. Whenever we find New Testament writers adding the qualification "of the dead" to the term "resurrection", the word "dead" is always a plural, never a singular. The "new earth in which righteousness dwells" (2 Peter 3:13) and the "new Jerusalem" where God will dwell with his people (Revelation 21:2-3, 10-14) will teem with inhabitants. It is therefore appropriate to observe that the Christian doctrine of a future resurrection prevents an individualistic understanding of immortality. Where we disagree with the Bishop is regarding the participants in this resurrection. He believes that it is the destiny of all persons to be perfected individually and corporately in the consummated Kingdom of God and to share directly in the eternal divine life. This thoroughgoing universalism ignores the fact that there is to be a "resurrection leading to condemnation" as well as a "resurrection leading to life" (John 5:29; cf. Matthew 5:29-30; 10:28), a resurrection of the unjust as well as a resurrection of the just (Acts 24:15; Revelation 20:4-5, 11-15). All persons, both the living and the dead, are subject to a future divine judgment (Acts 10:42; 2 Timothy 4:1; Hebrews 12:23) whose outcome will be determined on two bases: a person's relation to Christ (Matthew 7:22-23; Mark 8:38; John 3:36; 2 Thessalonians 1:8-9), and his or her works (Romans 2:6; 1 Peter 1:7; Revelation 20:12-13). Not all verdicts in this judicial investigation will be positive. Those who have refused to obey the gospel of the Lord Jesus and whose deeds are evil will suffer permanent banishment from God's presence (Romans 2:6, 8-9; 2 Thessalonians 1:8-9). A resurrection to eternal life is not the automatic destiny of every human being but a privilege God reserves for those who are related to Jesus Christ by faith and whose deeds display that faith (John 5:29; Romans 2:6-7, 10; 1 Corinthians 15:23, 52-54;

Galatians 5:5-6).

Finally, the Bishop rightly suggests that the full splendour of redeemed man's final state is beyond human knowledge. As John puts it: "What we shall be has not yet been revealed" (1 John 3:2). Agnosticism is misplaced, however, where the testimony of Scripture is clear. True, the New Testament writers show little concern for the geography of heaven or the anatomy and physiology of the resurrection body, but they do mention some of the characteristics of the spiritual body (e.g., it will be incapable of deterioration, beautiful in appearance, with limitless energy, and without sexual passions or procreative powers; Luke 20:35-36; 1 Corinthians 15:42-43; 2 Corinthians 5:1) and some of the privileges the righteous will enjoy in the hereafter (e.g., perpetual and direct sharing in the divine nature; bearing Christ's image; the vision, worship and service of God; reigning with Christ; sharing the divine inheritance; Romans 8:17, 29; 2 Peter 1:4; 1 John 3:2; Revelation 3:21; 5:10; 20:6; 22:3-5).

CONCLUSION

In all his writings Bishop Jenkins has consistently argued that Jesus' resurrection was God's act of perpetuating the presence and power of Jesus among his disciples after his death. Jesus rose, not bodily, from the grave, but spiritually (although none the less really), in the minds of the disciples. The basic flaw of such a view is that it confuses the nature and the effect of the resurrection. The disciples' emerging conviction that Jesus "was in fact not dead and finished, but alive and purposefully active" (*Glory*, p.32), was not itself the resurrection of Jesus but the result of the resurrection. According to the New Testament the resurrection of Jesus was his bodily and permanent emergence from death in a transformed state, and his exaltation to God's right hand. When the empty tomb and appearances of Jesus had made it clear that he had been reanimated and transformed, faith in the risen Jesus was born in his followers. We must never lose sight of the necessary distinction between the resurrection fact and the resurrection faith. "If Christ has not be raised, your faith is futile" (1 Corinthians 15:17): first the fact, then the faith. The disciples' faith in the risen Jesus derived its validity from the prior fact that Jesus rose from the dead.

What the Bishop offers us, then, is a sophisticated re-interpretation of the resurrection of Jesus. But it is not simply the case that a familiar theme has undergone an insignificant transposition of key. The tune itself is forfeited in this musical re-arrangement which cannot therefore be regarded as an acceptable interpretation of the New Testament score. What is in effect denied by the Bishop's views is (1) an Easter event that was experienced by Jesus himself, (2) a tomb that was empty because of the actual revival of the buried Jesus of Nazareth, (3) an individual existence of the risen Jesus in a spiritual body apart from his relation to the Church; and (4) a future resurrection of the unrighteous leading to their banishment from the divine presence.

But above and beyond these four specific doctrinal aberrations of the Bishop, there lurks the fundamental question of the nature of divine revelation and the authority of Scripture as a witness to and source of that revelation. One looks in vain through the Bishop's writings to find any expression of the

31

traditional view that God's special revelation is his self-disclosure in Jesus Christ and also in the Scriptures. Rather, "in its biblical and Christian form (or better, forms), the idea of revelation implies that men (some particular men, that is) have been enabled to form ideas, impressions and insights about the nature and possibilities of themselves and of the world under the particular guidance or influence of God" (*Man*, p.72). In keeping with this relativistic view of revelation, the Bishop sees his own theological writing as an exercise in experimental thought (*Glory*, pp.21,24,117). This explains why he frequently disclaims finality for his views, "these wonderings and wanderings of mine" as he expresses it in his 1969 "Easter meditation" on the resurrection (*Questions*, p.141). And in his most recent book (1976) he confesses at one point, with disarming frankness, "I am afraid of my arguing because it might be false and be so wholly a matter of fantasy and refusal to face realities that it is one more contribution to the confusing and misleading of human beings" (*Contradiction*, p.78). Precision of doctrine, he contends, is neither possible nor desirable. Thus a person may be regarded as a Christian who regards Jesus merely as a great moral teacher and a divine agent who leads people to God ("Credo"), or who holds the resurrection of Jesus to be symbolic, not factual (*Questions* p.136). It comes as no surprise, therefore, that although the Bishop's writings are punctuated at irregular intervals by allusions to biblical passages, Scriptural references or citations are exceedingly rare. The reader scarcely gains the impression either that "Holy Scripture contains all things necessary to salvation" (Article 6 of the Thirty-Nine Articles of Religion) or that it is one role of a Christian theologian to expound and defend its teaching.

In his views about the resurrection of Jesus, the Bishop has clearly failed to do justice to biblical teaching. Whatever assessment be made of his orthodoxy in other areas of belief, in this crucial area that is central to the Christian faith his views do not conform to the testimony of the New Testament in several important regards.